PIRATES

INFAMOUS PIRATES

KENNY ABDO

Fly!
An Imprint of Abdo Zoom
abdobooks.com

abdobooks.com

Published by Abdo Zoom, a division of ABDO, P.O. Box 398166, Minneapolis, Minnesota 55439. Copyright © 2022 by Abdo Consulting Group, Inc. International copyrights reserved in all countries. No part of this book may be reproduced in any form without written permission from the publisher. Fly!™ is a trademark and logo of Abdo Zoom.

Printed in the United States of America, North Mankato, Minnesota.
102021
012022

Photo Credits: Alamy, Getty Images, Granger Collection, Shutterstock
Production Contributors: Kenny Abdo, Jennie Forsberg, Grace Hansen
Design Contributors: Candice Keimig, Neil Klinepier, Laura Graphenteen

Library of Congress Control Number: 2021940194

Publisher's Cataloging-in-Publication Data

Names: Abdo, Kenny, author.
Title: Infamous pirates / by Kenny Abdo
Description: Minneapolis, Minnesota : Abdo Zoom, 2022 | Series: Pirates |
    Includes online resources and index.
Identifiers: ISBN 9781098226862 (lib. bdg.) | ISBN 9781644947012 (pbk.) |
    ISBN 9781098227708 (ebook) | ISBN 9781098228125 (Read-to-Me ebook)
Subjects: LCSH: Pirates--Juvenile literature. | Buccaneers--Juvenile literature. |
    Pirates--History--Juvenile literature. | Piracy--Juvenile literature.
Classification: DDC 910.4--dc23

TABLE OF CONTENTS

INFAMOUS PIRATES

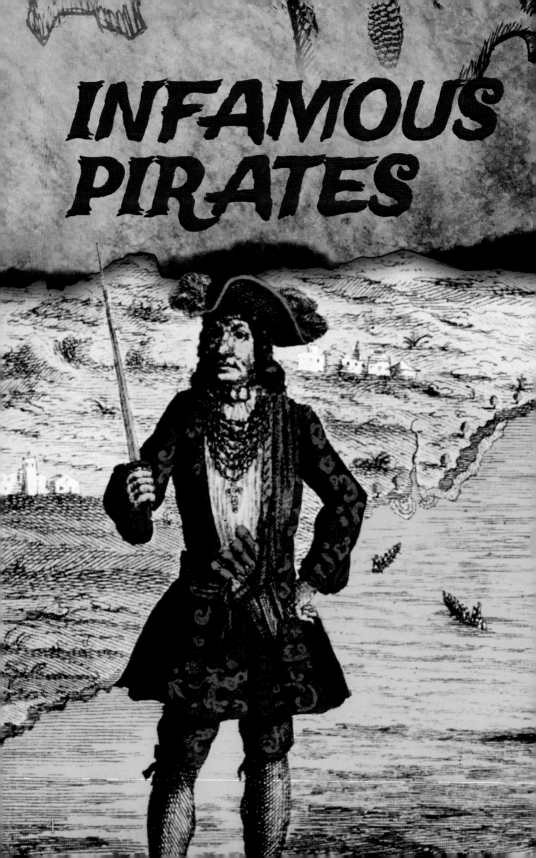

Jail breaking, rioting, and **plundering** were just a few of the things infamous pirates of the high seas liked to do.

From Blackbeard to Anne Bonny, notorious pirates have burned their legacies into history.

YE OLDE YARN

Many pirates began as **privateers**. They found **plundering** so profitable, they eventually went out on their own.

Though pirates have existed since ancient times, the **Golden Age of Piracy** was in the 17th and early 18th centuries. During this time more than 5,000 pirates were said to be at sea.

Some pirates were bloodthirsty.
Others were just greedy. But a few
were so successful, their names live
on in infamy.

VAST BOUNTY

EDWARD TEACH

B 47

Notorious pirate called "Blackbeard." Lived in Bath while Charles Eden was governor. Killed at Ocracoke, 1718.

ARCHIVES AND HIGHWAY DEPARTMENTS 1968

Blackbeard is known as the scariest pirate to ever live. Before taking a ship, Blackbeard would light fabric in his beard on fire. It made him look devilish. His victims swiftly gave up their fortunes.

Captain Henry Morgan ruled the
Caribbean seas first as a **privateer**.
He became a pirate in the mid-1600s.
Morgan is also known as one of the
few pirates to ever retire from piracy.

Sir Francis Drake circled the globe and defeated the **Spanish Armada**. He was also a feared pirate. The raids he led against the Spanish earned him some of the greatest bounties in pirating history.

Anne Bonny left her everyday life in
the early 1700s. Disguised as a man,
she joined Calico Jack Rackham's
crew. As history's most ruthless
female pirate, Bonny was feared by all
her male shipmates.

Calico Jack Rackham was famous for his grand robberies. He also designed the **Jolly Roger**. Captured in 1720, Rackham was strung up, tarred, and left as a warning to other pirates. That spot is now called Rackham's Cay.

Black Bart Roberts was one of the most successful pirates of the **Golden Age**. He robbed more than 400 **vessels** in just four years. Bart holds the record for most ships **pillaged** by a pirate in history.

Ching Shih was kidnapped from China in 1801. She eventually broke free and rose to power. Becoming one of the most dominating pirate captains, Shih eventually commanded a fleet of hundreds of ships.

Pirates are still active in places like the Indian Ocean, the Red Sea, and the coast of Somalia. But these modern-day robbers probably won't live on in infamy.

GLOSSARY

Golden Age of Piracy – a period between the 1650s and the 1730s when piracy was rampant in the Caribbean, the United Kingdom, the Indian Ocean, North America, and West Africa.

Jolly Roger – traditional flag flown by pirate ships indicating they were about to attack.

pillage – to raid a place or ship using violent means.

plunder – to steal goods and other things through violence and dishonesty.

privateer – a person who is sent by the government to carry out military missions, like robbing merchant ships and settlements.

Spanish Armada – a 130-ship fleet sent out by Spain to invade England in 1588.

vessel – a large boat.

ONLINE RESOURCES

Booklinks
NONFICTION NETWORK
FREE! ONLINE NONFICTION RESOURCES

To learn more about infamous pirates, please visit **abdobooklinks.com** or scan this QR code. These links are routinely monitored and updated to provide the most current information available.

INDEX